A Young Child's Bible

Copyright © 1997 Éditions Nathan, Paris, France

Printed in France. All rights reserved.

www.harperchildrens.com

Library of Congress Cataloging-in-Publication Data is available.

ISBN 0-06-029464-7

1 2 3 4 5 6 7 8 9 10

❖

First HarperCollins Edition, 2001

Original edition: *La Bible des petits*

Published in French by Éditions Nathan, 1997

Impression et reliure : Pollina s.a., 85400 Luçon - n° 80670

A YOUNG CHILD'S BIBLE

retold by
Élisabeth Gilles-Sebaoun

illustrated by
Charlotte Roederer

translated by *Joan Robins*

HarperCollins*Publishers*

CONTENTS

THE OLD TESTAMENT   5

The First Six Days   6

The Garden of Eden   9

Noah's Ark   15

The Tower of Babel   21

Abraham, Father of a Great People   23

Joseph in Egypt   26

The Israelites, the Pharaoh, and Moses   27

The Promised Land   39

God Sends the Prophets   44

The People of Israel Divided   50

THE NEW TESTAMENT   53

The Birth of Jesus   54

The Shepherds   58

The Three Wise Men   60

Jesus and the Temple of Jerusalem   62

The Baptism of Jesus   65

Jesus and His Disciples   67

The Parables   68

The Miracles   72

God Loves Children   76

Jesus Returns to Jerusalem   77

The Last Supper   78

Jesus on the Mount of Olives   79

The Judgment of Pontius Pilate   80

The Way of the Cross   81

The Crucifixion   82

The Resurrection   83

Jesus Returns   84

The Ascension   85

The Gift of the Holy Spirit   86

The Mission of the Disciples   87

Index of People and Places   88

THE OLD TESTAMENT

In the beginning, there was only God . . .

THE FIRST SIX DAYS

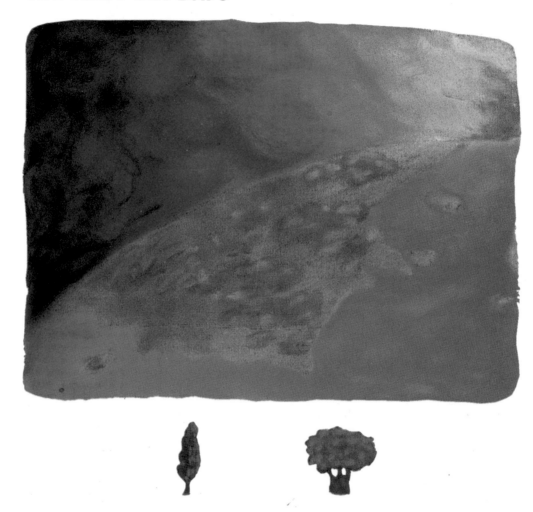

●

The Sky
and the Earth,
the Day
and the Night,
the Seas
and the Plants

There was no sky. There was no earth. There was no sun or moon. There were no people or animals, either. There was nothing, nothing at all. Only God existed. And God decided to create the world. So he brought forth the day and the night. He created the sky, the seas, and the land. And on the land he made thousands of plants grow: flowers, bushes, and trees of all kinds.

And then God created the sun, the moon, and the stars. It was beautiful, and God was pleased. But God had not yet finished his world. He also wanted to create thousands of animals. So he made birds for the sky, fish for the seas, and all kinds of creatures for the land.

Finally God decided to create a living being different from the animals—someone to look after them and to care for the land. And so God created man. He named him Adam. Now God's work was finished! It had taken him six days to create the world, and he was content with what he had made. On the seventh day God rested. That is why the seventh day is the day of rest, the day of God.

God made a marvelous paradise for Adam to live in: the Garden of Eden. Beautiful flowers and trees with the most delicious fruits grew there. And God had not forgotten water for the land: Four rivers flowed through the garden. God did all this so that Adam would be happy. Adam could live forever in the Garden of Eden and never be hungry or thirsty.

However, God warned Adam that he was not to eat the fruit of one tree, the tree planted in the center of the garden. If Adam tasted even one fruit from this tree, he would know what is good and what is evil, and one day he would die. Of course Adam promised never to touch the forbidden fruit.

God did not want Adam to be all alone, so he brought the animals to the Garden of Eden. He told Adam to find a name for each one. Adam named the monkey and the mouse, the rabbit and the goose, the zebra and the lion, the sheep, and many, many, others . . .

Adam was no longer alone then. Yet something was still missing. Every animal had a companion, but Adam did not. So God created woman. And Adam named her Eve.

●

Adam and Eve
in the Garden

Adam and Eve lived happily in the garden. They loved each other very much and were never apart. They lacked nothing and could do whatever they wanted: run in the grass, gather the flowers, eat the fruits, bathe in the rivers, and play with their friends the animals.

Adam and Eve had never known meanness or evil. They did not even know that evil existed. And yet evil, through the trickery of the serpent, destroyed the happiness of Adam and Eve.

One day the serpent mocked Eve because she did not dare to taste the fruit from the forbidden tree. The serpent told Eve that this fruit was so extraordinary that on eating it she would become as strong and intelligent as God himself. The fruit did look delicious! And instead of listening to God, Eve chose to listen to the serpent. She bit into the forbidden fruit, then asked Adam to do the same. And Adam, too, took a bite of the fruit.

As soon as they had tasted the fruit, Adam and Eve felt ashamed of being naked. They were so embarrassed that they covered themselves with leaves. And when God called to Adam in the garden, Adam tried to hide.

God knew immediately what had happened. He was very angry! He gave Adam and Eve clothes made from animal hides, and he made them leave the marvelous garden . . .

Later, Adam and Eve had children. Time passed. The children grew up and, in their turn, had children.

A very long time after Adam and Eve, there were a great many men and women on earth. But they seemed to have forgotten God. They behaved terribly and fought among themselves. Seeing their meanness, their jealousy, and their selfishness made God very sad. Evil was everywhere! He was sorry that he had created man. Mankind had become bad.

God decided to destroy mankind in a giant flood. He would make so much rain fall that the seas, the lakes, and the rivers would overflow, covering all of the land.

But God knew there was one man who was worth saving, a man who was good and generous, and who had always kept God in his heart. This man was called Noah.

●

Noah Builds
the Ark and
Gathers the
Animals

God ordered Noah to build an immense boat, an ark, where Noah and his family could take shelter from the flood. Noah did exactly what God asked of him. Night and day he worked with his sons to build the ark.

God also ordered Noah to gather a male and female of each of the many animals that he had created. As soon as the ark was finished, Noah had all the animals come on board—furred animals and feathered animals, animals that walk and animals that fly, those that crawl and those that jump; the tiny, the big, and the ones in between.

Finally, with his wife, and his sons and their wives, Noah entered the ark. And God himself closed the door.

Seven days later a torrential rain began to fall on the land. Soon the ark began to float. The water continued to rise and rise. The trees disappeared and still the water rose. And then the mountains, too, disappeared.

Finally the rain stopped. It had lasted forty days and forty nights. But the flood was not yet over. Now they had to wait until the water went down. And so Noah waited.

The Raven
and the Dove

Noah waited a long time. Then he let out a raven. But the raven returned quickly to shelter in the ark. The water was still there, everywhere, and the bird had not found any land to rest on. After a while Noah let a dove out, but in a few hours it, too, returned. One morning he let the dove fly off again. This time it reappeared in the evening, very late, and in its beak it carried a tiny branch from an olive tree. Noah then knew that plants had begun to grow again somewhere on earth. Noah waited some more. Then the dove flew off one last time. The bird never returned. It must have found a young tree in which to make its nest.

Noah knew that the moment had come to leave the ark. He opened the door and let out the two beavers, the two rabbits, the two geese, the two foxes . . . and all the other animals. Then Noah and his family left the ark. They were grateful to be on solid ground again. The earth was sparkling clean and smelled so good. Their first steps on land filled them with joy.

Noah thanked God. And God made a promise to Noah: Never again would he destroy mankind, even if people behaved badly to one another. Suddenly a rainbow appeared in the sky. God had created it just for Noah to show that he would keep his promise. This rainbow was the sign of God's love and commitment to Noah and all the living creatures of the earth.

THE TOWER OF BABEL

The children of Noah had many children, and later, in their turn, the grandchildren of Noah had children. So it was that people could once again be counted by the thousands. All of these people spoke the same language. One day they went forth to settle on a big plain. They decided to build a beautiful city with a tower so high that it would go all the way up to the sky. Men had learned to make bricks that were strong and solid; they were proud of themselves and felt powerful. They began to build. Soon the tower almost reached the clouds.

But God thought that mankind had become much too proud. He had given them the land and now they wanted the sky, too! So to stop them, God made them all speak different languages. Now they could no longer understand one another's words. And as they could not talk to each other, they could not work together to finish the tower. They went their separate ways and settled all over the earth. The tower they abandoned is called Babel.

ABRAHAM, FATHER OF A GREAT PEOPLE

Among men there were many who had forgotten God, but Abraham was one who loved God with all his heart. One day God ordered Abraham to leave his house and his father. He wanted to give Abraham a rich land where he would prosper. And Abraham obeyed.

He set out on a long journey with his wife, Sarah, his servants, and his herds of animals. Guided by God, Abraham arrived at last in the country of Canaan.

God gave this land to Abraham, who settled there. Then God told him that he would have a son. Abraham was very surprised because he thought he and Sarah were much too old to have a child. However, nothing is impossible for God. He wanted to make a special bond with Abraham and to be his friend forever. God promised Abraham that he would be the father of a great people.

A year later, just as God had said, Sarah gave birth to a son. At God's request, the baby was named Isaac.

Isaac grew into a young boy. Then God asked
Abraham to do something very difficult: to offer his son to
him. God had given a son to Abraham and now he wanted
him back. Abraham was unhappy, but he obeyed. He led
his son to a very high mountain. But as he was preparing
to give his son back to God, an angel stopped him.

In fact, God never had intended to take back Isaac.
He had just wanted to see if Abraham loved him so much
that he would even offer him his only son. And God blessed
Abraham, who then sacrificed a ram instead of his son
to God.

JOSEPH IN EGYPT

Joseph Sold
by His Brothers

Isaac grew up and had twin sons, Esau and Jacob. Jacob was so courageous and strong that God gave him a new name, Israel. Later, Israel had twelve sons! One of them, Joseph, was his father's favorite, and his brothers were terribly jealous. Wanting to be rid of Joseph, they sold him to merchants who took him to Egypt. There, with God's help, Joseph became governor of the pharaoh's lands.

Then there was a terrible drought, even in Canaan, where Joseph's eleven brothers still lived. Soon there was nothing to eat. Joseph asked his brothers to come settle with him in Egypt, where he had stored food for seven years. Thus the twelve sons of Israel were happily reunited.

THE ISRAELITES, THE PHARAOH, AND MOSES

Many years passed. The descendents of Israel were now so numerous in Egypt that they formed a great people, the Israelites.

But one day the new pharaoh began to worry. The Israelites were becoming too important. These strangers were of the Hebrew tribe. Egypt was not their country. And, worst of all, they were powerful and therefore dangerous!

The Israelites
Become Slaves

The pharaoh ordered the Israelites to do the most difficult work, without pay. He made slaves of them! They had to build roads and houses from morning to night. Egyptian guards watched over them, ready to whip them if they stopped working. But the Israelites were strong and became ever more numerous. That made the pharaoh so angry that he gave a terrible order: All newborn Israelite boys were to be thrown into the great river Nile!

One Israelite baby escaped this sad fate. His mother
had successfully hidden her little boy for three months.
Then, terrified that he would be discovered, she put her
baby in a basket that she placed at the edge of the river,
hiding it in the reeds. She hoped that God would come to
her son's aid. That very day the pharaoh's daughter came
to the bank of the river to bathe. Suddenly she spotted the
basket. She peeked into it and discovered the baby.

The pharaoh's daughter knew immediately that the baby was Hebrew, but her heart was so touched, so moved, that she said nothing about it to her father. How could she throw this baby into the Nile? She kept her discovery a secret. She gave the baby to a nursing mother so that he would have milk. Then, when he was big enough, the pharaoh's daughter brought the child to her palace. She gave him a name, Moses, which means "saved from the waters."

The daughter of the pharaoh raised Moses as her own son—like an Egyptian. But as he grew, Moses learned that he was a child of the people of Israel. And soon he discovered that his people were treated badly.

One day Moses saw an Egyptian beating an Israelite. Moses threw himself immediately on the Egyptian and killed him. When the pharaoh learned of this, he sent his guards to find Moses and kill him. But Moses fled to another country, and there he settled down and married.

One night, as Moses was watching over his sheep, he saw a fire in the middle of a bush. He came nearer and then stopped, amazed. Despite the flame, the bush was not burning. Suddenly Moses heard a voice. It was the voice of God. And God told Moses that he must go to the pharaoh and ask him to let the Israelites leave Egypt. Next, Moses was to lead his people to Canaan, the country of his ancestors Abraham, Isaac, and Israel. God promised to help him. If the pharaoh refused, terrible disasters would strike Egypt!

As God had ordered, Moses returned to Egypt to ask the pharaoh to let the Hebrew people go. The pharaoh refused. He did not even believe in this God of whom Moses spoke! Moses asked the pharaoh several times. And to make the pharaoh give in, Moses showed him what God was capable of doing.

This is what happened: First the water in the river changed to blood; then frogs invaded Egypt, hopping right into people's houses; finally millions of mosquitoes and horseflies bit all the Egyptians, even the pharaoh. But the pharaoh stubbornly refused to give in.

The Pharaoh
Allows the
Israelites to
Leave

A sickness then killed the Egyptians' herds. That was followed by an epidemic of boils. Then there was a terrible hailstorm! Next, clouds of grasshoppers ate up all the plants. Then a pitch-black night covered all of Egypt. It lasted three days! But the pharaoh, even though he was very frightened, still refused to free the Israelites. Moses then told him that the eldest child of every Egyptian family—including the pharaoh's own—would die in the night, but that the angel of death would pass over the houses of the Israelites, and their children would live.

Finally, after this terrible thing happened, the pharaoh allowed the Israelites to leave.

God had freed the people of Israel. And to be sure they never forgot this event, God commanded each Israelite family to honor the occasion by eating a special meal with unleavened bread, as their bread would not have time to rise before they left Egypt. And thereafter they were to eat the same meal each year in memory of the night in which God had shown his power. He gave it a name: the feast of Passover—or *Pesach* in Hebrew.

Guided by God, Moses led the Israelites out of Egypt. But when the pharaoh realized that there would no longer be any slaves to build his houses, he wanted them back and sent his army after them. The Israelites soon saw Egyptian warriors with their armed chariots coming up behind them. And before them lay the Red Sea. They were trapped and they trembled with fear! Then God told Moses to raise his staff over the sea. Moses obeyed. The sea divided in two, leaving a passage for the amazed Israelites. When they reached the other side, Moses held up his hand, and the sea closed in on the pharaoh's soldiers. The Israelites thanked God for saving them.

The Israelites continued their journey. They marched for a long time in the desert. Soon they complained to Moses—they were hungry and thirsty. God heard them and looked after them so that they would not suffer. Each morning the ground was covered with a kind of white powder that tasted of honey. It was delicious to eat and was called manna. And for the hot and thirsty, Moses had only to hit a rock with his staff and water poured forth immediately!

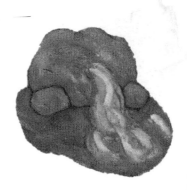

The Israelites had arrived at the foot of a mountain in the desert of the Sinai. One morning the mountain trembled. There were deafening claps of thunder and clouds of smoke. The Israelites were terrified. Moses knew that God awaited him, and he climbed the mountain. God gave him tablets of stone engraved with laws, the Ten Commandments. God was the friend of the people of Israel, but there were rules that had to be respected, such as to love God, not to lie, not to steal, not to kill, and other rules as well . . .

After a journey of forty years, at long last the people of Israel returned to Canaan, the promised land. Moses had died of old age some time before they arrived.

Little by little the Israelites began to live happily in Canaan. They even chose a king, Saul. But during his reign the Israelites had frequent wars with enemies such as the Philistines.

One day, when the armies of the Israelites and the Philistines got ready to attack each other, a Philistine warrior stepped out of the ranks and proposed to fight alone against one Israelite soldier. If he won, the Israelites would become slaves of the Philistines.

This warrior, who was called Goliath, was a gigantic man, bigger than a bear, stronger than a lion. King Saul was very worried because no one could win against such a giant! However, a young shepherd, David, offered to fight him. David had no fear. He said that God was with him. In fact, David was the very man God had chosen to become king after Saul.

David refused Saul's armor and sword. The young shepherd came before Goliath to do battle with nothing but some stones and his sling. These were enough for David.

The giant, Goliath, wore heavy armor and held his awesome sword as if it were an enormous lance. When he saw David, he burst out laughing. How could someone so small, so ridiculous, challenge him? He wasn't even armed!

But David had great faith in God. He approached the metal-clad colossus, put a stone in his sling, and let it go with all his strength. The stone hit Goliath's forehead, and he crumbled heavily onto the ground. David then seized Goliath's great sword and cut off his head. When the Philistines saw that their champion was dead, they fled.

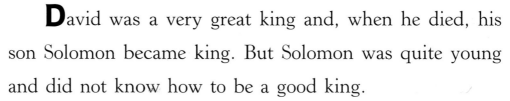

David was a very great king and, when he died, his son Solomon became king. But Solomon was quite young and did not know how to be a good king.

One night, in a dream, God asked Solomon what he wished for most. Solomon replied that he wanted to be a wise king who was just and good. So God made Solomon a great wise man, and he also gave him riches and glory. Never was there a king wiser or more just than Solomon.

One day two women with a baby came before King Solomon. Both claimed to be the baby's mother. Solomon proposed that the women divide the baby between them. But that meant the baby would have to be cut in two!

One of the women immediately agreed to dividing the baby. But the second woman, with a cry of despair, refused and begged that the baby be given to the other woman instead. Thus Solomon knew who the true mother was: the one who had begged him not to harm her child, even though it meant she had to give him up.

GOD SENDS THE PROPHETS

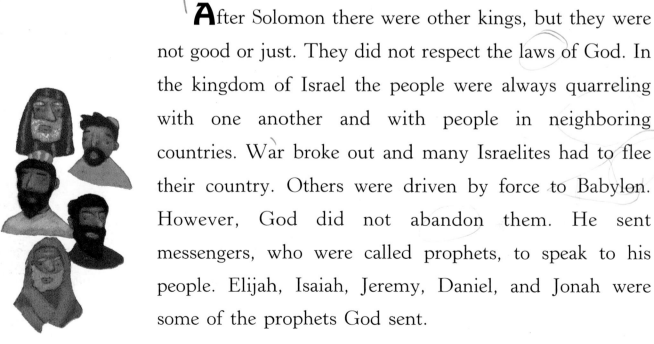

After Solomon there were other kings, but they were not good or just. They did not respect the laws of God. In the kingdom of Israel the people were always quarreling with one another and with people in neighboring countries. War broke out and many Israelites had to flee their country. Others were driven by force to Babylon. However, God did not abandon them. He sent messengers, who were called prophets, to speak to his people. Elijah, Isaiah, Jeremy, Daniel, and Jonah were some of the prophets God sent.

Daniel, an Israelite, lived in Babylon. The king of Babylon, Darius, was Daniel's friend. But some ministers of the court were jealous of the men's friendship and wanted to get rid of Daniel. So they persuaded Darius to make a new law: For thirty days, no one would have the right to pray to a god. Anyone who did so would be thrown to the lions. Of course Daniel continued to love and to pray to God. When King Darius was told this, he had to punish Daniel. That made him unhappy because he loved Daniel.

The evening before Daniel was to be thrown into the lions' den, Darius begged his friend to pray to God to be saved. That night Darius was so upset that he was unable to eat or sleep. The next morning he rushed over to the lions' den, crying, "Daniel, has your god protected you from the lions?" And Daniel, alive and well, replied that God had sent some angels who had closed the mouths of the lions. Darius was very happy. Daniel was freed, and the jealous ministers were thrown into the den and eaten by the lions.

Jonah Flees
by Boat

Like Daniel, Jonah was also chosen to be God's messenger. But at first, Jonah did not want to do what God asked of him. This is what happened: God, who had had enough of the wicked behavior of the Assyrians, ordered Jonah to go to their big city, Nineveh. Jonah refused, because he did not like the people of Assyria. And he tried to escape on a boat.

Jonah
Swallowed by
an Enormous
Fish

God was angry. He caused a tremendous storm on the sea. The boat was in danger of sinking, and the sailors and passengers were very frightened. Jonah realized that the storm was his fault. God was displeased with his behavior. Jonah told the captain that he must throw him overboard to stop the tempest. So the sailors threw Jonah into the sea and God ended the storm immediately.

But just then an enormous fish threw itself upon poor Jonah and swallowed him whole. For three days and three nights, Jonah remained a prisoner in the belly of the fish.

Jonah asked pardon of God and the fish spit Jonah out onto the shore. Jonah then went to Nineveh. He ran through the city giving God's message to its people: They had to stop being wicked or God would destroy their city in forty days. The Assyrians were amazed that Jonah's God cared how they behaved. They regretted the bad things they had done and asked for God's pardon. As for Jonah, he realized that God loved not only the people of Israel but also the people of Assyria. God loves all peoples.

The Romans
Invade the
Promised Land

God had chosen prophets to tell people what he expected of them: "Stop doing bad things. Be good to one another! Be just and wise!" However, there were many who did not stop being bad and there were many wars. Because of all the fighting, the land of Israel had been abandoned by many Israelites. Then the Romans, a strong and powerful people, invaded it. They gave the land of Israel a new name: Palestine.

Most of the Israelites who had remained in Palestine lived in the southern part of the country, the region of Judea. Thus the Israelites were called Jews.

The Jews did not like living under the Romans. However, they had not forgotten that God had made them a promise. He had sent a prophet, Isaiah, to tell them of the birth of a king! But not a king to command a country or make war! No! This was a king who would have the spirit of God in his heart, a king full of love. This was a king for all times, a king for all peoples. And the Jews longed for the coming of this king. They awaited the king God promised them, the king they called the Messiah.

THE NEW TESTAMENT

God fulfills his promise . . .

THE BIRTH OF JESUS

Mary and
Joseph

Mary was a sweet and kind young woman. Her home was in Nazareth, a little village in Galilee, a province located in northern Palestine. Mary lived simply and she was very happy. Soon she would be marrying her fiancé, Joseph.

Then one day God sent her a messenger, the angel Gabriel.

When the angel Gabriel appeared in Mary's home, she was amazed and troubled. Gabriel talked to Mary. He told her that God had chosen her to be the mother of a little boy, whom she was to call Jesus. Jesus would be king and his reign would never end. Mary was confused. How could she be going to have a baby when she was not even married to Joseph yet? The angel Gabriel then explained that the power of God, the Holy Spirit, would come to her. That is why this baby would be holy and called the Son of God.

Mary was filled with wonder. Soon she would be the mother of the Son of God! The mother of the Messiah!

A short time later, the emperor of the Romans wanted to know how many people lived in his empire. Each man was ordered to appear with his family in the city where he had been born. There, his name, and the names of his wife and children, would be written down.

Mary was now married to Joseph. They left for Bethlehem, the city where Joseph had been born, to be registered there. Mary was expecting a baby, as the angel Gabriel had foretold. A donkey carried her because her child was soon due.

On the evening they arrived in Bethlehem, Mary felt that her baby was ready to be born. But there were no vacant rooms at the inns. Joseph was very worried. He ran around the city looking for shelter for Mary. At last he found a stable in which some animals were sleeping. And it was there, that night, that Mary had her baby. She wrapped him tenderly in linens and laid him on the straw of a manger.

THE SHEPHERDS

This same night, God sent an angel to some shepherds who were watching over their sheep not far from Bethlehem. The night sky was suddenly filled with a dazzling light. They were frightened! Then, in the midst of this light, an angel appeared. And the angel said he had marvelous news for them: A baby had just been born in Bethlehem, and this child was the Messiah. The angel told the shepherds that they would find the baby lying in a manger.

The shepherds left immediately for Bethlehem and quickly found the stable where the baby slept. As soon as they saw little Jesus, the Son of God, they loved him with all their hearts and knelt down before him. In the days that followed, the shepherds told everyone that the Messiah promised by God had finally arrived, and they had seen him!

THE THREE WISE MEN

But God wished to show that Jesus was not only king of the Israelites. He was the king of all people in all nations! So God sent a sign to other people far away to let them know of the coming of the Messiah. He made a very bright star appear in the sky of a distant country in the East. In this country lived three great wise men, the magi.

The three magi followed the star of God to Bethlehem, where they found the infant Jesus. Their hearts filled with joy, the magi got down on their knees and adored the child of God. Then the rich magi offered the baby sumptuous gifts of gold, frankincense, and myrrh. Thus God showed that Jesus loved all people, whether near or far, poor as the shepherds, or rich as the magi.

JESUS AND THE TEMPLE OF JERUSALEM

Joseph, Mary, and Jesus went back to live in their little house in Nazareth. Jesus was growing up. He was now a kind and helpful young boy, and people loved him. When he was twelve years old, Mary and Joseph took him to Jerusalem to celebrate Passover. They went to pray in the temple, the house of God.

After the celebration of Passover, they set off for home. Each year more and more people came to Jerusalem to celebrate Passover, and there were many people on the road.

Mary and Joseph were trudging along with all the others when suddenly they realized Jesus was not with them. Had he run ahead with the other children? Mary and Joseph searched for him in the crowd. They asked people if they had seen their little boy. But no one had! Jesus had disappeared! Mary and Joseph, terribly upset, walked all the way back to Jerusalem to look for Jesus.

Finally, after three days, they found him. Jesus was sitting in the temple of God! He was talking with some very wise old men. Jesus was asking them questions and listening to their answers. And these masters of the law of God were very impressed by the intelligence and wisdom of the young boy.

Mary asked her son, "Why did you do this? We were so worried." And Jesus answered, "Why did you have to search for me? Where would I be but in the house of my Father?" Mary and Joseph did not understand what Jesus meant but were happy he was safe and sound. All three set off again on the road to Nazareth.

John the

Baptist

The years passed. In the desert of Judea, not far from Jerusalem, lived a man called John the Baptist. Every day he baptized people in the water of the river Jordan. And he told them that the Messiah was going to come. He asked each of them to be good, to be gentle, to do no evil, and to love God. When John baptized the Jews in the water, it was as if he had washed away their faults.

One day John the Baptist saw a man approaching him who wished to be baptized. Immediately he recognized Jesus, the Messiah, and he baptized him in the river. It was a very great honor for John the Baptist. When Jesus came out of the water, the Spirit of God descended upon him in the form of a dove. At that very moment the voice of God was heard to say, "Thou art my beloved son."

JESUS AND HIS DISCIPLES

Jesus went one day to the Sea of Galilee. There he saw two men fishing, Simon and his brother Andrew. Jesus asked them to follow him. He needed them to teach people to know and love God, his Father. The two men followed Jesus at once. Jesus then called two other fishermen, James and his brother John. These four were the first of the twelve disciples of Jesus.

With his disciples, Jesus traveled throughout the country. He explained to people they should be good to one another. And to be sure that they would understand his message, Jesus told them beautiful stories, the parables.

One day a man said to Jesus, "God asks me to love my neighbor, but who is my neighbor?" Jesus did not answer this question directly, but told him this parable instead: There was once a Jew who was attacked on a road by thieves. They hit him very hard and took his money. The poor wounded man lay on the ground. A priest passed by but did not help him. A servant passed near him, but he, too, did nothing for the man. The wounded man felt miserable. No one came to help him.

Then he saw a Samaritan approach with his donkey. For a long time the people of Samaria had been enemies of the Jews. So the wounded man was sure that this Samaritan would never come to his aid. However, it was the Samaritan who offered help. He took care of the man's wounds, lifted him onto his donkey, and led him to an inn.

The Samaritan had given proof of a generous spirit toward the Jew, his neighbor. Jesus said to the man who had questioned him, "Go and you, too, do the same."

Jesus told another parable to explain the meaning of generosity and pardon:

The son of a very rich farmer asked his father one day to give him a lot of money because he wanted to go to another country. The father agreed and the son left.

In this other country, the son feasted day and night. He spent all his money on beautiful clothes and food. Soon he had nothing left. He looked after a farmer's pigs in exchange for a bit of food.

Miserable and starving, the son finally returned home to his father. He begged his father to pardon him and to let him return as a servant. But his father welcomed him tenderly and held a big celebration in his honor. The eldest son, who had remained with his father and worked hard for him, became angry. After all, his younger brother had behaved terribly. But his father asked him to understand that his brother had learned a lesson and to share the father's joy in having regained his son!

THE MIRACLES

Sometimes Jesus did the most extraordinary things to show the power of God—he performed miracles. He cured the sick; he restored sight to the blind. He even brought people who were dead back to life. Many people had heard tell of this marvelous man who spoke of God's love and who accomplished miraculous things.

When Jesus arrived with his disciples in the city of Capernaum, people rushed to see and hear him.

Some men carrying a paralyzed man on a stretcher tried to reach Jesus, but there were too many people around him. So they climbed on the roof of a house and lowered the stretcher down close to Jesus. The paralyzed man believed that Jesus would be able to cure him. Jesus bent over the man who could not walk and said to him, "Get up and walk!" And this man who believed very strongly in God raised himself from his stretcher and walked. When Jesus cured those who were unfortunate, it showed that God loved them.

One morning Jesus crossed the Sea of Galilee with his companions. On the shore a big crowd awaited him. There were thousands of people who wished to hear the words of Jesus. He spoke to them for a long time, until night fell. Everyone was hungry, but there was nothing to eat!

Jesus and his disciples had brought only five little loaves of bread and two fish with them. Yet Jesus asked his disciples to feed the crowd.

How was this possible? There were five thousand people! But Jesus blessed the five little loaves and the two fish and then shared them. The sharing went like this: a bit of bread and a little fish for you, a bit of bread and a little fish for you, too . . . Somehow there was always more—a bit of bread and a little fish—for the disciples to give each person! And after everyone's hunger was satisfied, there was still enough food to fill a dozen baskets!

GOD LOVES CHILDREN

One day some people brought their children to see Jesus. But the disciples tried to send them away. They did not want Jesus to be bothered by children. But Jesus said to them, "Let the children come as close to me as they want!" The disciples obeyed. Jesus welcomed the children. He blessed them and took them in his arms and on his knees. Then he explained to the disciples that children, and all of the small and the weak, are as important to God as the big and the strong.

JESUS RETURNS TO JERUSALEM

Jesus and his disciples returned to Jerusalem to celebrate Passover. A crowd welcomed him with cheers. People cried, "Blessed be he who comes in the name of the Lord!" Many people believed that Jesus was the Son of God. But some priests did not. Nor did they believe that he was the Messiah sent by God. Jesus knew that he had some dangerous enemies and that they wanted to have him arrested by the Roman soldiers. Jesus also knew that he was going to have to suffer and to die before rejoining his Father.

THE LAST SUPPER

Jesus Shares
the Bread
and the
Wine

The first day of Passover, Jesus and his disciples came together for the supper. During the meal, Jesus shared the bread, blessing it and handing it to his disciples. Then Jesus announced that he was going to die the very next day.

He explained that his body, which he was giving up for love of mankind, was a little like the bread that he had just shared. And he explained that his blood, which would be spilled for love of mankind, was a little like the wine that he had also just shared.

JESUS ON THE MOUNT OF OLIVES

After the supper, Jesus went with his disciples to the Mount of Olives. There, in a grove of olive trees, he prayed. If Jesus was the Son of God, he was also a man. And as a man he was afraid of suffering, afraid of dying.

Suddenly, a troop of soldiers threw themselves on Jesus and arrested him. The disciples were so frightened that they ran away.

THE JUDGMENT OF PONTIUS PILATE

The next day, Jesus was led before Pontius Pilate, the Roman governor who commanded the province of Judea. Pilate did not understand why the Jewish priests wanted to get rid of Jesus. Why kill him? What wrong had he done? But the priests accused Jesus of claiming to be the Son of God! So Pilate told the priests that they must decide what should be done. And the priests demanded that Jesus be put on a cross as was done with criminals. The soldiers then led Jesus away and he was beaten.

THE WAY OF THE CROSS

81

●

Jesus Carries

the Cross

It was said that Jesus thought he was the king of the Jews! So to mock him, the Roman soldiers dressed him in a purple mantle such as kings wore. And they placed a crown on his head. But this crown was not made of gold; it was made of thorns. And then the soldiers put a cross on his shoulders for him to carry all the way to Golgotha. But the cross was so heavy that Jesus had trouble carrying it. A soldier ordered a man to help Jesus. A crowd of people watched the passing of Jesus and his cross. Women who knew Jesus well cried.

THE CRUCIFIXION

When he arrived at Golgotha, Jesus was put on the cross. The people who passed by made fun of him: "If you are the Son of God, get yourself down from the cross!" But Jesus said: "Father, pardon them, because they do not know what they do." Then, at the very moment that Jesus died, night fell instantly and the earth trembled!

After Jesus' death, his body was taken off the cross. He was wrapped in a large white sheet, then put in a tomb that looked like a cave. An enormous stone was rolled in front of the entrance to seal the tomb.

Three days later, Mary Magdalene, a woman who had known Jesus well, went to the tomb. She saw that it had been opened—and that the body of Jesus had disappeared!

As she was crying in front of the tomb, a man approached her. He was smiling and told her not to be sad. He called her by her first name, Mary. And then she recognized him. It was Jesus!

Immediately Mary ran to announce the good news to the disciples: Jesus was no longer in the tomb. He had come back to life! He was alive again, and she had seen him!

JESUS RETURNS

Jesus came to see the disciples several times. The first time he came, they were very surprised. They were together in a house with the doors and windows closed when suddenly Jesus was there, too! At first they were very scared. Was this a phantom? But a phantom does not eat! And Jesus had eaten with them.

The last time that Jesus came to visit the disciples, he announced that they were soon going to be visited by the Spirit of God, a great force full of love. And, because of this love, the disciples would be able to announce throughout the world that Jesus the Messiah had come and that the kingdom of God existed for everyone.

Then Jesus rose into the heavens and disappeared. He had rejoined his Father.

THE GIFT OF THE HOLY SPIRIT

When the disciples were together on the day of the Jewish festival of the harvest, the Pentecost, they suddenly felt a strong gust of wind and saw little flames come down and rest on each of their heads. It was the force, the Spirit of God, that Jesus had promised them. At that very instant, the disciples became capable of speaking all the languages of the world. And so it was that in each country where they went they were understood.

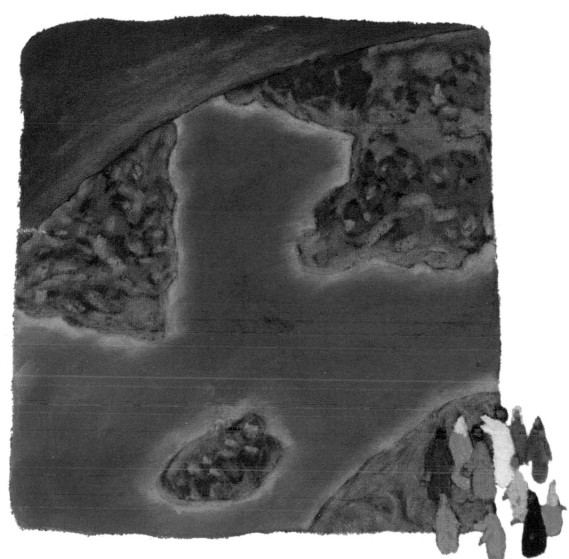

The disciples of Jesus set out across the whole world to tell the story of Jesus, the Son of God.

He, Jesus, was the Messiah promised by God. And he had come to tell all men that God loved them and that they must all love one another.

INDEX OF PEOPLE AND PLACES

Abraham, 23–25, 32

Adam, 8–14, 15

Andrew, 67

Assyria, 47, 49

Babel, 21–22

Babylon, 44–45

Bethlehem, 56–57, 58–59, 61

Canaan, 23, 26, 32, 39

Capernaum, 72

Daniel, 44–47

Darius, 45–46

David, 40–42

Egypt, 26, 27, 32–36

Elijah, 44

Esau, 26

Eve, 11–14, 15

Gabriel, 54–56

Galilee, 54

Golgotha, 81, 82

Goliath, 40–41

Isaac, 24–25, 26, 32

Isaiah, 44, 51

Israel, *see* Jacob

Israel (nation), 32, 35, 39,
    44, 49, 50–51

Jacob (renamed Israel), 26, 27,
    32
James, 67
John, 67
John the Baptist, 65–66
Jeremy, 44
Jerusalem, 62–63, 65, 77
Jesus, 55, 59, 60–61, 62–64,
    66, 67, 68–70, 72–75, 76, 77,
    78, 79, 80, 81, 82, 83, 84,
    85, 86, 87
Jonah, 44, 47–49
Jordan, 65
Joseph (husband of Mary),
    54–56, 62–64
Joseph (son of Israel), 26
Judea, 51, 65, 80

Mary, 54–57, 62–64
Mary Magdalene, 83
Moses, 29–34, 36–38, 39
Mount of Olives, 79

Nazareth, 54, 62, 64
Nile, 28, 30
Nineveh, 47, 49
Noah, 15–20, 21

Palestine, 50–51, 54
Pontius Pilate, 80

Red Sea, 36

Samaria, 69
Sarah, 23–24
Saul, 39–40
Sea of Galilee, 67, 74
Simon, 67
Sinai, 38
Solomon, 42–43, 44